Knock Knock

180 Stupendously Silly Knock Knock jokes
to make your kids laugh all day long!

Try Not
To Laugh!

Copyright of Matt Woods
& The Joke Station

Our Best-Selling Book...

Click here to buy now

Knock knock.
> **Who's there?**

Troy.
> **Troy who?**

Troy not to laugh at my jokes!

Knock knock.
> **Who's there?**

Cash.
> **Cash who?**

No, it's almonds.

Knock knock.
> **Who's there?**

Candice.
> **Candice who?**

Candice day get any worse?

Knock knock.
    Who's there?
Boo.
    Boo who?
Now, now. It's okay.

Knock knock.
    Who's there?
Dewey.
    Dewey who?
Dewey have any chocolate?

Knock knock.
    Who's there?
Lettuce.
    Lettuce who?
Lettuce play outside!

Knock knock.

Who's there?

Razor.

Razor who?

Razor hands if you want treats.

Knock knock.

Who's there?

Iran.

Iran who?

Iran so fast when I saw my mom!

Knock knock.

Who's there?

Howl.

Howl who?

Howl I sneak outside to play?

Knock knock.
    Who's there?
Needle.
    Needle who?
I needle bit more time!

Knock knock.
    Who's there?
Thermos.
    Thermos who?
Thermos be food at home.

Knock knock.
    Who's there?
Water.
    Water who?
Water you up to today?

Knock knock.
>Who's there?
Dozen.
>Dozen who?
Dozen anyone have a pen?

Knock knock.
>Who's there?
Amish.
>Amish who?
Amish you too!

Knock knock.
>Who's there?
Annie.
>Annie who?
Annie way, I have to go now.

Knock knock.
> **Who's there?**

Nana.
> **Nana who?**

Nana of you can beat me!

Knock knock.
> **Who's there?**

Ben.
> **Ben who?**

Ben waiting for you!

Knock knock.
> **Who's there?**

Spell.
> **Spell who?**

That's easy. W. H. O.

Knock knock.
> **Who's there?**

Yule.
> **Yule who?**

Yule never know unless you try.

Knock knock.
> **Who's there?**

Canoe.
> **Canoe who?**

Canoe hear what I'm saying?

Knock knock.
> **Who's there?**

Juno.
> **Juno who?**

Juno how much ice cream I ate?

Knock knock.
    Who's there?
Olive.
    Olive who?
Olive you too!

                    Knock knock.
                        Who's there?
                    Alec.
                        Alec who?
                    Alec your smile!

Knock knock.
    Who's there?
Orange.
        Orange who?
Orange you going to sleep yet?

Knock knock.
>Who's there?

Figs.
>Figs who?

Figs your hair, it's messy!

Knock knock.
>Who's there?

Zany.
>Zany who?

Is Zany one in the room?

Knock knock.
>Who's there?

Noice.
>Noice who?

Noice to meet you.

Knock knock.
Who's there?
Ho-ho.
Ho-ho who?
Santa, is that you?

Knock knock.
Who's there?
Dishes.
Dishes who?
Dishes a beautiful house you have.

Knock knock.
Who's there?
Mikey.
Mikey who?
I lost Mikey! Can you let me in?

Knock knock.
> **Who's there?**

Witches.
> **Witches who?**

Witches the way to the store?

Knock knock.
> **Who's there?**

Jess.
> **Jess who?**

I like your Jess!

Knock knock.
> **Who's there?**

Tyrone.
> **Tyrone who?**

Tyrone as fast as you can.

Knock knock.
    Who's there?
Iva.
    Iva who?
Iva bad habit of being lazy.

Knock knock.
    Who's there?
Scold.
    Scold who?
Scold in here, isn't it?

Knock knock.
    Who's there?
Watson
    Watson who?
Watson your mind
lately?

Knock knock.

Who's there?

Noah.

Noah who?

Do you Noah a great place to eat?

Knock knock.

Who's there?

Leaf.

Leaf who?

Please don't leaf me here!

Knock knock.

Who's there?

Butter.

Butter who?

Slow down! Butter be careful.

Knock knock.
>Who's there?

CD.
>CD who?

CD ant on the floor? It's so small.

Knock knock.
>Who's there?

Who.
>Who who?

Is there an owl?

Knock knock.
>Who's there?

Ears.
>Ears who?

Ears another great pun for you!

Knock knock.
> Who's there?

Ferdie.
> Ferdie who?

Ferdie please, more sweets!

Knock knock.
> Who's there?

Althea.
> Althea who?

Althea soon buddy!

Knock knock.
> Who's there?

Cher.
> Cher who?

Cher would like some cake?

Knock knock.
> Who's there?

Iona.
> Iona who?

Iona new bike, check it out!

Knock knock.
> Who's there?

Alex.
> Alex who?

Alex-plain later!

Knock knock.
> Who's there?

Keanu.
> Keanu who?

Keanu help me out?

Knock knock.
> **Who's there?**

Lion.
> **Lion who?**

Stop lion on the floor, it's dirty!

Knock knock.
> **Who's there?**

Stopwatch.
> **Stopwatch who?**

Stopwatch you're doing right now!

Knock knock.
> **Who's there?**

Hike.
> **Hike who?**

Sorry, I'm not good with peotry.

Knock knock.
> Who's there?

Haven.
> Haven who?

Haven you had enough of puns?

Knock knock.
> Who's there?

Luke.
> Luke who?

Hey, Luke out!

Knock knock.
> Who's there?

Anita.
> Anita who?

Anita to have a haircut.

Knock knock.
Who's there?
Tennis.
Tennis who?
Tennis eight plus two.

Knock knock.
Who's there?
Nun.
Nun who?
Nun of it makes sense.

Knock knock.
Who's there?
Sweden.
Sweden who?
Sweden sour crispy pork!

Knock knock.
   Who's there?
Ice cream soda.
   Ice cream soda who?
Ice scream soda you can hear me!

Knock knock.
   Who's there?
Cereal.
   Cereal who?
It's cereal pleasure to meet you!

Knock knock.
   Who's there?
Odysseus.
   Odysseus who?
Odysseus the last slice of cake!

Knock knock.
        Who's there?
June.
        June who?
June know what month it is?

                        Knock knock.
                                Who's there?
                        You.
                                You who?
                        Yes, I can see you!

Knock knock.
        Who's there?
Allison.
        Allison who?
Allison to the song you suggested.

Knock knock.
Who's there?
Hawaii.
Hawaii who?
Hawaii you doing there?

Knock knock.
Who's there?
Adore.
Adore who?
Please close Adore for me.

Knock knock.
Who's there?
Aida.
Aida who?
Aida lot of food today!

Knock knock.
    Who's there?
Turnip.
    Turnip who?
Can you turnip the music? I like it.

Knock knock.
    Who's there?
Icing.
    Icing who?
Icing really good! Did you know?

Knock knock.
    Who's there?
Police.
    Police who?
Police tell me you're joking!

Knock knock.
> **Who's there?**

Abby.
> **Abby who?**

Abby birthday buddy!

Knock knock.
> **Who's there?**

Double.
> **Double who?**

Do you mean W?

Knock knock.
> **Who's there?**

Gladys.
> **Gladys who?**

I'm Gladys the weekend already!

Knock knock.

> **Who's there?**

Theodore.

> **Theodore who?**

Don't forget to close Theodore!

Knock knock.

> **Who's there?**

Yah.

> **Yah who?**

No, I prefer google.

Knock knock.

> **Who's there?**

Snow.

> **Snow who?**

Snow use going on a diet!

Knock knock.
 Who's there?
Closure.
 Closure who?
Closure eyes and make a wish.

Knock knock.
 Who's there?
Gorilla.
 Gorilla who?
Gorilla burger. I've got buns!

Knock knock.
 Who's there?
Abbot.
 Abbot who?
Abbot you let me play outside?

Knock knock.
  Who's there?
Owls say.
  Owls say who?
Yes, you just did.

Knock knock.
  Who's there?
Hatch.
  Hatch who?
Oh, Bless you!

Knock knock.
  Who's there?
Europe.
  Europe who?
No! you are!

Knock knock.
Who's there?
Quiche.
Quiche who?
Can I quiche you on the cheek?

Knock knock.
Who's there?
Lena.
Lena who?
Lena little closer and I'll tell you a secret!

Knock knock.
Who's there?
Conrad.
Conrad who?
Conrad-ulations! You aced it!

Knock knock.
>Who's there?

Dwayne.
>Dwayne who?

Dwayne the pool! My toy sunk.

Knock knock.
>Who's there?

Smell mop.
>Smell mop who?

Ew! That's gross.

Knock knock.
>Who's there?

Ida.
>Ida who?

I think it's pronounced as Ida-ho.

Knock knock.
  Who's there?
Kenya.
  Kenya who?
Kenya hear me now?

Knock knock.
  Who's there?
Avenue.
  Avenue who?
Avenue seen this movie?

Knock knock.
  Who's there?
Harry.
  Harry who?
Please Harry up!

Knock knock.
> Who's there?

Mustache.
> Mustache who?

Mustache some goodies later.

Knock knock.
> Who's there?

Cabbage.
> Cabbage who?

A cabbage doesn't have a last name!

Knock knock.
> Who's there?

Cow.
> Cow who?

Can you cow me later?

Knock knock.

Who's there?

A herd.

A herd who?

A herd you were looking for me?

Knock knock.

Who's there?

Alfie.

Alfie who?

Alfie tried already.

Knock knock.

Who's there?

Anee.

Anee who?

Do you need Anee-thing?

Knock knock.
Who's there?
Roach.
Roach who?
Roach you a poem, aren't I sweet?

Knock knock.
Who's there?
Ketchup.
Ketchup who?
Long time no see. Let's ketchup!

Knock knock.
Who's there?
Norma Lee.
Norma Lee who?
Norma Lee I'm a funny person.

Knock knock.
> **Who's there?**

Viper.
> **Viper who?**

Viper face, you're a mess.

Knock knock.
> **Who's there?**

Amos.
> **Amos who?**

Look! Amos-quito.

Knock knock.
> **Who's there?**

Yukon.
> **Yukon who?**

Yukon count on me!

Knock knock.
Who's there?
Abbot.
Abbot who?
Abbot time you wake up!

Knock knock.
Who's there?
Sherwood.
Sherwood who?
Sherwood be nice to be taller.

Knock knock.
Who's there?
Honeydew.
Honeydew who?
Honeydew to help me exercise!

Knock knock.
    Who's there?
Oink oink who.
    Oink oink who who?
Are you an owl or a pig?

Knock knock.
    Who's there?
A pile up.
    A pile up who?
Yuck! Thats gross.

Knock knock.
    Who's there?
Wooden shoe.
    Wooden shoe who?
Wooden shoe say that I'm smart?

Knock knock.
Who's there?
Doris.
Doris who?
Can you let me in? Doris locked.

Knock knock.
Who's there?
Ada.
Ada who?
Ada great sleep last night!

Knock knock.
Who's there?
Barbara.
Barbara who?
Barbara black sheep, have you any wool?

Knock knock.
Who's there?
Sadie.
Sadie who?
Just Sadie magic word!

Knock knock.
Who's there?
Justin.
Justin who?
Justin time for breakfast!

Knock knock.
Who's there?
Claire.
Claire who?
Hurry! Claire the way!

Knock knock.
   Who's there?
Beats.
   Beats who?
I love chocolate beats's in cookies.

Knock knock.
   Who's there?
Nobel.
   Nobel who?
There's Nobel, so I just knocked.

Knock knock.
   Who's there?
Ale.
   Ale who?
Ale let you play outside later!

Knock knock.
  Who's there?
Donut.
  Donut who?
Donut ask me, I donut know either.

Knock knock.
  Who's there?
Alpaca.
  Alpaca who?
Alpaca sandwich for you now.

Knock knock.
  Who's there?
Nuisance.
  Nuisance who?
Cut your nails to keep your nuisance.

Knock knock.
  Who's there?
Barbie.
  Barbie who?
I love Barbecues!.

Knock knock.
  Who's there?
Frank.
  Frank who?
Frank you for asking.

Knock knock.
  Who's there?
Howard.
  Howard who?
Howard I know? I just arrived.

Knock knock.
> **Who's there?**

Kanga.
> **Kanga who?**

It's pronounced kanga-roo!

Knock knock.
> **Who's there?**

Icy.
> **Icy who?**

Yes, I see you too.

Knock knock.
> **Who's there?**

Otto.
> **Otto who?**

Can you take me Otto here?

Knock knock.
Who's there?
Joe.
Joe who?
I love to Joe around and laugh!

Knock knock.
Who's there?
Ken.
Ken who?
When Ken I open my gifts?

Knock knock.
Who's there?
Wendy.
Wendy who?
Let me know Wendy the game is over, I want to join the next one.

Knock knock.
Who's there?
Tank.
Tank who?
No problem, you're welcome!

Knock knock.
Who's there?
Kent.
Kent who?
Kent you tell that it's me?

Knock knock.
Who's there?
Chick.
Chick who?
Can you please Chick the mail?

Knock knock.
    Who's there?
Goat.
    Goat who?
I'll goat to the park. Want to come?

Knock knock.
    Who's there?
Some bunny.
    Some bunny who?
Some bunny has been very lazy!

Knock knock.
    Who's there?
Wired.
    Wired who?
I feel kinda wired after all that sugar!

Knock knock.
  Who's there?
Mary.
  Mary who?
I think you're too young for that.

Knock knock.
  Who's there?
Irish.
  Irish who?
Irish I could see you!

Knock knock.
  Who's there?
Nose.
  Nose who?
I think he Nose more jokes than me.

Knock knock.
   Who's there?
Amarillo
   Amarillo who?
Amarillo nice person, you know!

Knock knock.
   Who's there?
Havana.
   Havana who?
I'm havana great weekend!

Knock knock.
   Who's there?
Juneau.
   Juneau who?
Juneau where to buy cupcakes?

Knock knock.
> **Who's there?**

Cheese.
> **Cheese who?**

Cheese a very pretty lady.

Knock knock.
> **Who's there?**

Andrew.
> **Andrew who?**

Andrew a portrait of you.

Knock knock.
> **Who's there?**

Irene.
> **Irene who?**

Irene need to take a bath.

Knock knock.
Who's there?
Oslo.
Oslo who?
Time is moving Oslo right now.

Knock knock.
Who's there?
Bed.
Bed who?
Bed you cant beat me in a race.

Knock knock.
Who's there?
Burglars.
Burglars who?
Burglars don't knock on doors!

Knock knock.
Who's there?
Cargoes.
Cargoes who?
Everyone knows cars go BEEP!

Knock knock.
Who's there?
Abel.
Abel who?
The name doesn't really ring Abel.

Knock knock.
Who's there?
Ivene.
Ivene who?
Ivene really wanting to take a bath.

Knock knock.
> **Who's there?**

Alice.
> **Alice who?**

Alice well and good.

Knock knock.
> **Who's there?**

Venice.
> **Venice who?**

Venice she coming home?

Knock knock.
> **Who's there?**

Kiwi.
> **Kiwi who?**

Kiwi go to the mall later?

Knock knock.
> **Who's there?**

Radio.
> **Radio who?**

Radio not, here I come!

Knock knock.
> **Who's there?**

Mae.
> **Mae who?**

Mae be I'll tell you later.

Knock knock.
> **Who's there?**

A little old lady.
> **A little old lady who?**

You didn't tell me you could yodel!

Knock knock.
   Who's there?
Zoo.
   Zoo who?
Zoo do you think this is?

Knock knock.
   Who's there?
Hannah.
   Hannah who?
Could you Hannah piece of paper?

Knock knock.
   Who's there?
Linda.
   Linda who?
I'll Linda hand if you need one!

Knock knock.
>**Who's there?**
Cactus.
>**Cactus who?**
It's raining cactus dogs!

Knock knock.
>**Who's there?**
Heidi.
>**Heidi who?**
Heidi-cided to sleep early!

Knock knock.
>**Who's there?**
Roonie.
>**Roonie who?**
Stop Roonie so fast, I cant catch up.

Knock knock.

> **Who's there?**

Baby owl.

> **Baby owl who?**

Baby owl see you later then?

Knock knock.

> **Who's there?**

Ghost says.

> **Ghost says who?**

No, ghosts say boo!

Knock knock.

> **Who's there?**

Bach.

> **Bach who?**

Wake up! I have a Bach of cakes.

Knock knock.
> **Who's there?**

Bacon.
> **Bacon who?**

I'll be bacon cookies for your Dad!

Knock knock.
> **Who's there?**

Voodoo.
> **Voodoo who?**

Voodoo you think I am?

Knock knock.
> **Who's there?**

Jess.
> **Jess who?**

It's Jess me, myself and I.

Knock knock.
> **Who's there?**

Barry.
> **Barry who?**

Hurry up and Barry the treasure!

Knock knock.
> **Who's there?**

Kermit.
> **Kermit who?**

Be careful not to Kermit a crime!

Knock knock.
> **Who's there?**

Cook.
> **Cook who?**

I didn't know you were a bird.

Knock knock.
Who's there?
Wire.
Wire who?
I don't know, wire you asking me?

Knock knock.
Who's there?
Hada.
Hada who?
Hada great time! How about you?

Knock knock.
Who's there?
Sorry.
Sorry who?
Sorry! Wrong door.

Knock knock.
  Who's there?
Fiddle.
  Fiddle who?
Fiddle make you happy, I'll do it.

Knock knock.
  Who's there?
Jim.
  Jim who?
Jim mind if I come in?

Knock knock.
  Who's there?
Jamaica.
  Jamaica who?
Did Jamaica a mistake?

Knock knock.
Who's there?
Grub.
Grub who?
Grub a hold of my hand!

Knock knock.
Who's there?
Bruce.
Bruce who?
Got to be careful, I Bruce easily.

Knock knock.
Who's there?
Emma.
Emma who?
Emma really getting tired of all these puns!

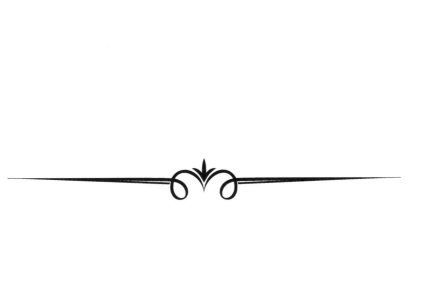

If you enjoyed laughing over book with your children, please leave a positive review on Amazon...

We love seeing how much you love our collection of joke books!

Our Best-Selling Book...

Click here to buy now

New books Coming soon!

The Joke Station

THE JOKE STATION

+ Follow

Follow to get new release updates and improved recommendations

Side-splitti... ...hole family. Keep you... ...ed for hours and hours... ...ou... ...ection!

We publish joke... ...s & gam... ...ooks from the most c... ...e and hilarious minds of today.

£3.99
Kindle Edition

Books By The Joke Station

All Formats | Kindle Books | Pape

Stay up to date

Printed in Great Britain
by Amazon